Cookies, Cream And "Me"

Written by
Artice Coleman

Cookies, Cream And "Me"

Copyright © 2024 by Artice Coleman. All rights reserved.

No part of this publication may be reproduced, distributed, or transmitted in any form or by any means, including photocopying, recording, or other electronic or mechanical methods, without the prior written permission of the author, except in the case of brief quotations embodied in critical reviews and certain other noncommercial uses permitted by copyright law.

The contents of this work, including, but not limited to, the accuracy of events, people, and places depicted; opinions expressed; permission to use previously published materials included; and any advice given or actions advocated are solely the responsibility of the author, who assumes all liability for said work and indemnifies the publisher against any claims stemming from publication of the work.

Printed in the United States of America
ISBN 978-1-64133-942-1 (sc)
ISBN 978-1-64133-943-8 (e)
ISBN 978-1-64133-944-5 (hc)

2024.10.02

This book is printed on acid-free paper.

Because of the dynamic nature of the Internet, any web addresses or links contained in this book may have changed since publication and may no longer be valid. The views expressed in this work are solely those of the author and do not necessarily reflect the views of the publisher, and the publisher hereby disclaims any responsibility for them.

BlueInk Media Solutions
1111B S Governors Ave
STE 7582 Dover,
DE 19904

www.blueinkmediasolutions.com

Special Thanks

I want to thank my son Remaro and my daughter-in-law Danielle for giving me such a blessingm and my grandson Tristan and all the joy that comes wrapped within him. May God bless you all and for making me feel some kind of special. Becoming a grandmother and the anticipation of spreading my love beyond ways that I could not even imagine. What a mighty God we serve. God Bless with real love wrapped around it.

Coco Grammy

The color of my skin is very unique mommy and daddy blended together, I am better than a peach.

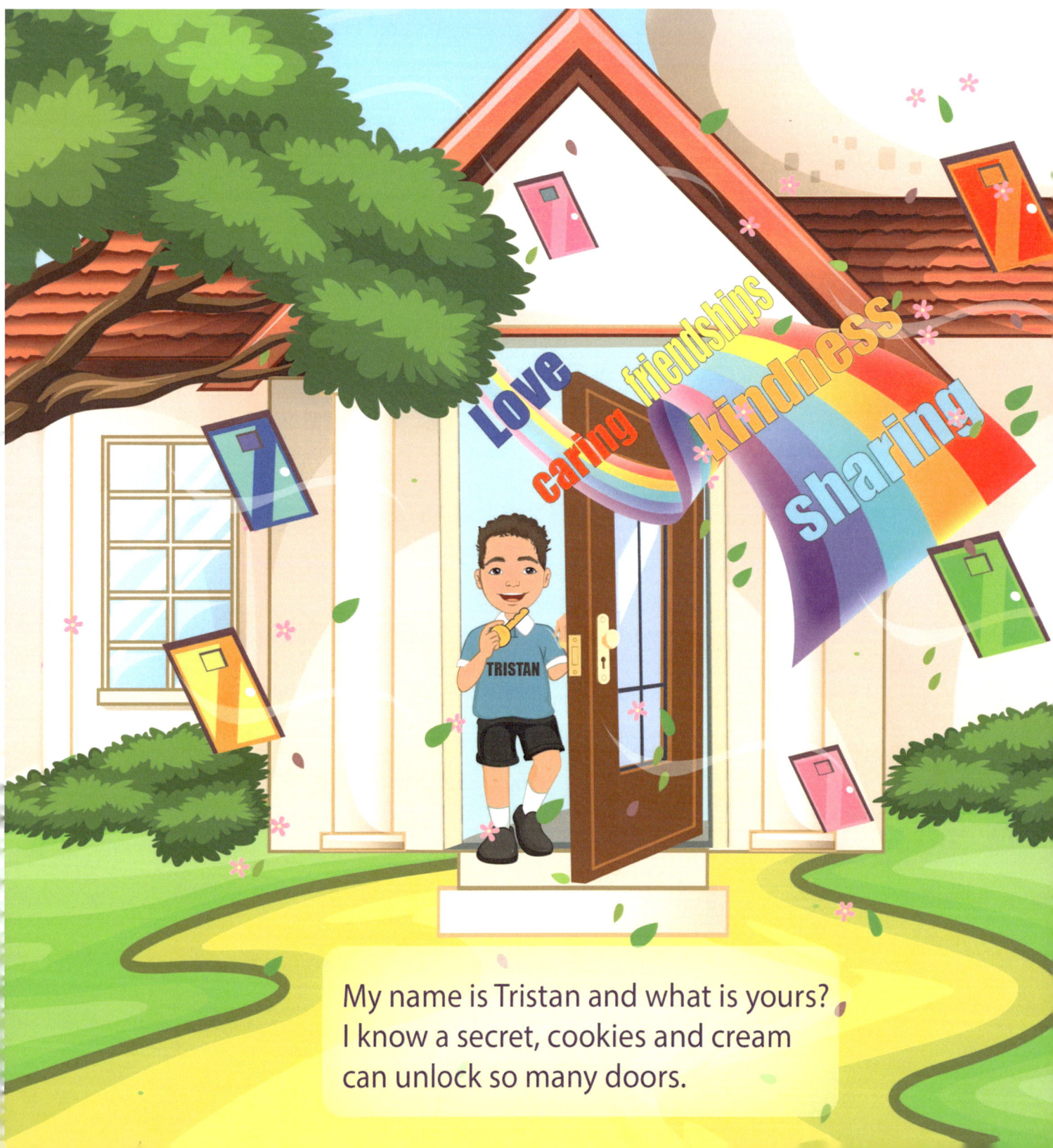

Is based on a little boy named Tristian, who is biracial and because of the color of his mom and dad's skin, it gives him a unique color concerning his skin type. And because of the society we live in, there will be more and more blended families, that we all will encounter, which makes *Cookies, Cream, And "ME"* to be added to your little one's library in making it special and relatable, for a time such as this!

I am truly blessed to be able to create a book such as this. I'm a wife, mother and now bless to becoming a grandmother and a great grandmother and the little one in the story line, belongs to me. He's one of eight grandchildren and four great grandchildren. There are two mottos that I lived by, one is "Life can be great if you don't weaken", and the other one "when you have children of your own one day, your life will be the only pages they glean from, that will determine their success in life". People are important to me especially the little ones that are in this world, remember, no matter the color of your skin and the families that you are born in, you can do all things and by knowing that, nothing is impossible for you to do and to reach for those things that have been placed within your imagination and you are special in the eyes and hands of God!

With true love wrapped around it!
Artice Coleman
Author

www.ingramcontent.com/pod-product-compliance
Lightning Source LLC
LaVergne TN
LVRC091352060526
838200LV00016B/366